TopReaders

The Silk Road

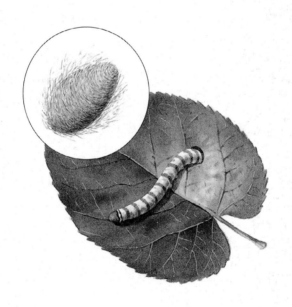

Robert Coupe

Contents

In ancient China, silk was a precious material. Over time, traders from China moved westward as far as Europe and Africa. They traded silk and other products. The routes on which they traveled are now called the Silk Road.

Venice

The Silk Road

In 1272, young Marco Polo, with his father and uncle, set out from Venice, Italy. For three years, they traveled, by sea and over land, to China. They followed a route that we now call the Silk Road. Centuries earlier, traders from China first moved along this route.

Marco Polo traveled by camel across the harsh Gobi Desert. This was one of the most difficult parts of the Silk Road.

Gobi Desert

CHINA

INDIA

☆ **Map Key**
— going to Asia
— coming home
— traveling in China

Starting Out

For centuries, the ancient Chinese did not move away from China. But 2,000 years ago, they began to travel to new lands. They needed to find strong horses for their army. Over time, these travelers started to trade silk and other products in far-off places.

☆ Money in China

Ancient Chinese coins had holes in the middle. They were carried on a piece of string or cord. This made it easy to carry and count large sums of money.

Chinese traders set up camp in the desert as they traveled toward the west.

Reaching Europe

Traders from China began moving westward. They traveled across northern India and through the Middle East . Two centuries later, trade routes reached as far as Constantinople. This city is the place where Asia ends and Europe begins.

Fact File

More than 1,700 years ago, Constantine I moved the capital of the Roman Empire to Byzantium. Constantine changed the name of the city to Constantinople.

Istanbul is the modern name of Constantinople. It is now the largest city in Turkey.

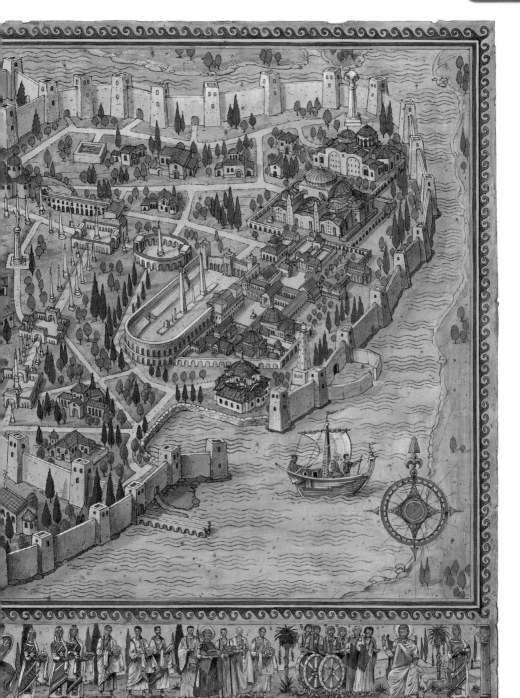

Arab Traders

About 1,200 years ago, Arab traders from the Middle East were traveling long distances by both land and sea. Laden with goods, their ships sailed eastward to India and southern China. In large groups, called caravans, traders moved over land through Africa and Asia.

Baghdad is now the capital of Iraq. In earlier times, its narrow, dusty streets were lined with traders.

Arab Ships

Arab merchants sailed in timber vessels called dhows. They had sails shaped like large triangles. Dhows had sharp, high bows and moved swiftly through the water.

What Was Traded?

Silk was the main product that Chinese merchants took on their trade journeys. They also took painted wooden goods, tea, and spices. They exchanged these for gold, silver, and other luxury materials.

Chinese and Arab traders often met up in the desert and traded goods there.

Fact File

In 139 BC, Zhang Qian traveled to central Asia to buy horses. He returned with lots of facts about countries to China's west.

☆ Spinning Cocoons

After they hatch from eggs, young silkworms feed on mulberry leaves. Then they spin their cocoons .

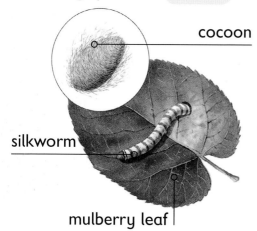

cocoon

silkworm

mulberry leaf

Making Silk

Silk is made from the thread silkworms spin to make their cocoons. Women in ancient China wove this thread to make silk cloth. People in other places did not learn to make silk until much later. Traders sold silk for very high prices.

People gathered mulberry leaves to feed to silkworms. Women rinsed the cocoons in hot water to loosen the thread.

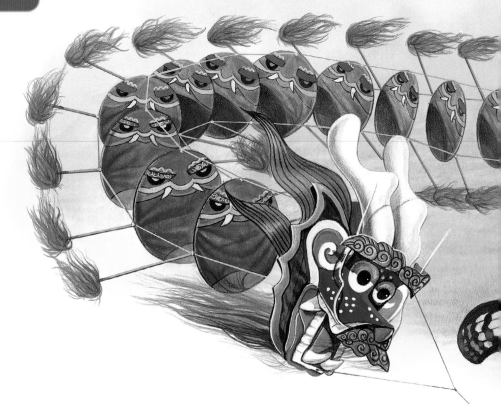

People in ancient China loved to make and fly kites.
At first, kites were made of silk and bamboo. Later,
paper, which was lighter, was used instead of silk.

Uses for Silk

Silk in ancient China was used mainly to make clothes.
It is still widely used today as a fabric for fine clothing.
Rich Chinese women often wore shoes made of silk.
Chinese artists wove different-colored silk threads
into tapestries that showed scenes from nature.

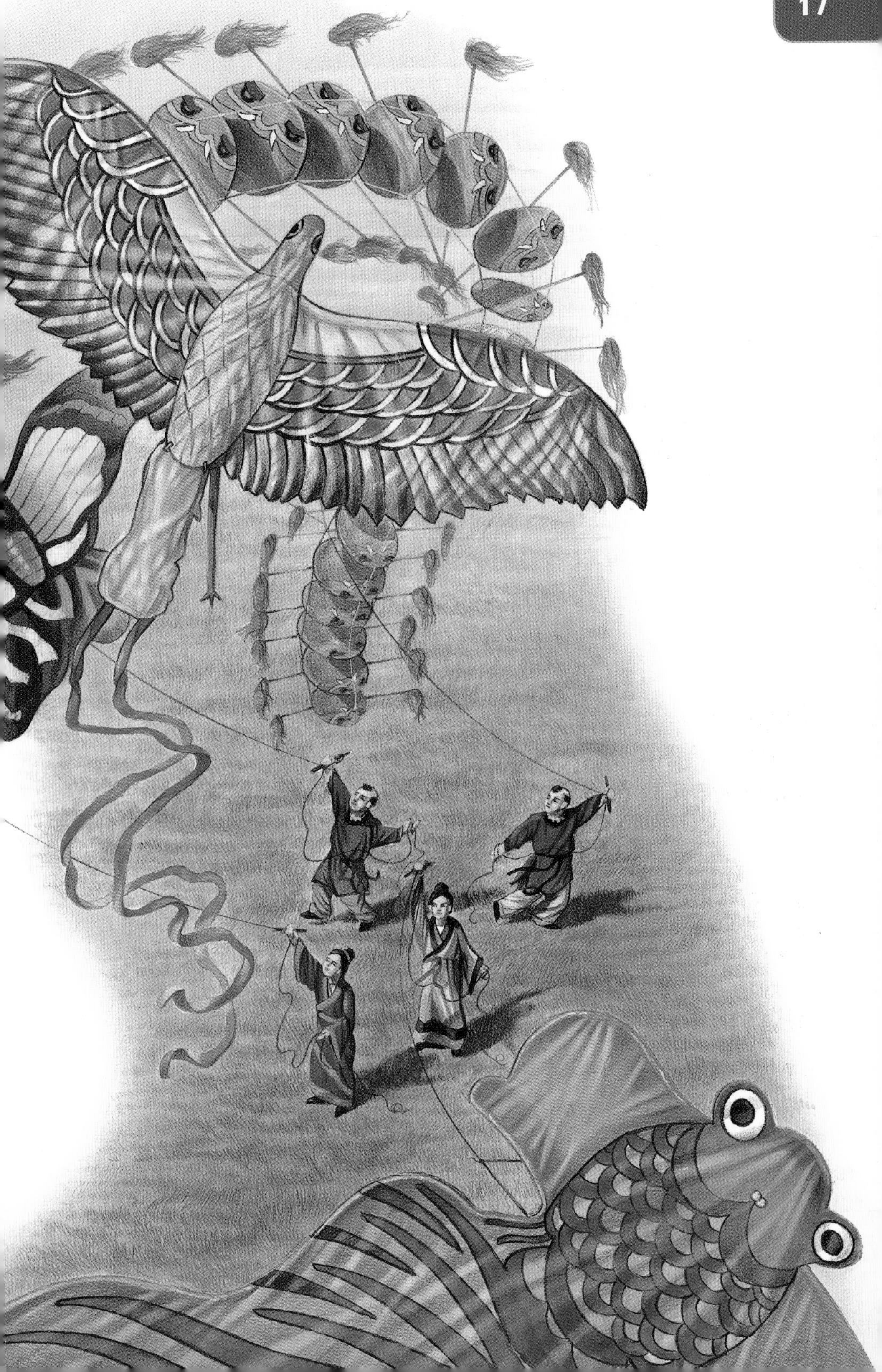

Silk Clothes and Paintings

Rich people in ancient China dressed in silk clothes when they were in public. Silk was expensive. At home, they wore less costly garments. Rich women often wore jewelry of jade , gold, silver, and brass. Poorer people wore hemp clothes and copper and iron jewelry.

Silk Paintings

Many modern artists paint on canvas. Artists in China often painted on silk, coated with a substance called alum . Flower and bird pictures were very popular.

Rich Chinese women wore long skirts and loose jackets with short sleeves. Men wore long, loose robes that had wide, heavy sleeves.

As trade developed, *ambassadors* from foreign countries exchanged costly gifts with Chinese emperors.

Emperors

For more than 300 years, China ruled the world's largest empire. Emperors lived in great luxury. They were praised in good times, but blamed if droughts or other bad events happened.

Voyages and Gifts

In 1406, a Chinese admiral, Zheng He, sailed from China. He commanded a huge fleet of ships. They carried large cargoes of silk, tea, and porcelain . The fleet went as far as Africa. The Chinese gave gifts to people they met and brought back many goods.

Fact File

Chinese porcelain was the finest in the world. Chinese traders sold porcelain to rich people in Europe.

Zheng He brought back some very unusual presents from Africa. One of them was a giraffe, which he presented to the emperor.

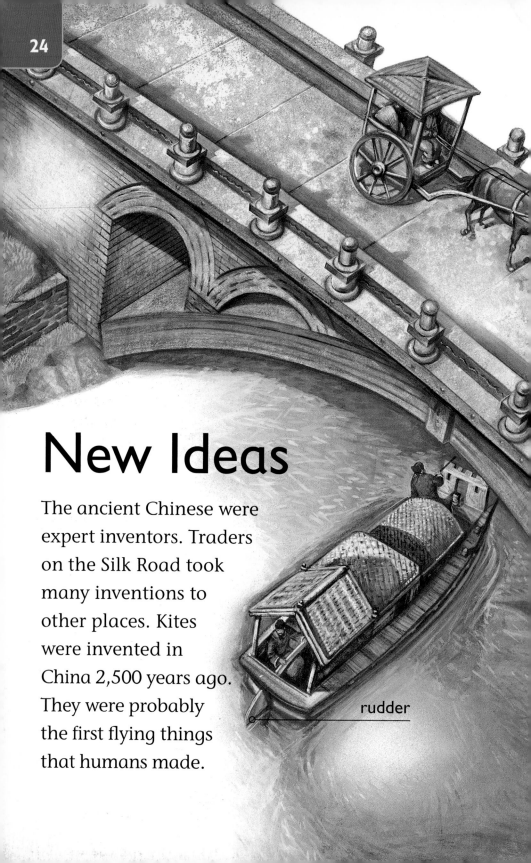

New Ideas

The ancient Chinese were
expert inventors. Traders
on the Silk Road took
many inventions to
other places. Kites
were invented in
China 2,500 years ago.
They were probably
the first flying things
that humans made.

rudder

kite

umbrella

fishing reel

The picture shows some of the things that the Chinese invented.

wheelbarrow

New Religions

In ancient China, Confucius was a great religious leader. Laozi was another leader. He founded the Daoist religion. The third great ancient Chinese religion was Buddhism. Buddhism began in India about 2,500 years ago. It reached China about 200 years later.

Confucius

 Buddhist Bells

Bells, like the ones shown here in Tibet, play an important part in Buddhist religious ceremonies.

Early traders along the Silk Road brought Buddhism to China. Later on, people from Europe and the Middle East introduced Christianity and other religions into China.

Buddha

Laozi

The Silk Road Today

Over the centuries, new and better ships were developed. More and more goods moved between countries by sea. By the 1500s, the land routes that led from China to Europe and Africa were no longer used for trade. Many tourists now move along the old Silk Road.

Hotan

Hotan is on the Silk Road between China and India. It is still an important center of silk production. More than 1,000 people in Hotan now make silk there.

The city of Jiayuguan was a stopping point on the Silk Road. This fort near the city is now a popular place for tourists to visit.

⭐ ☆ **Fact File**

This fort at Jiayuguan was built in the 1500s, when trade along the Silk Road was almost at an end.

Quiz

Can you unscramble the words and match them with the right pictures?

WIMSLORK   WHOD

EKTI   DHUBAD